COLLISIONS OF THE HEART

COLLISIONS OF THE HEART

Curtis Jones

Acknowledgement

First I give all honor to my heavenly Father (YHWH) for making a way for me everyday.

I want to acknowledge my wife, my Beautiful one, Christina Jones, for all her Love, support, and inspiration. I love you for life.

I would definitely have to give honor and thanks to My Mama Bessie Jones. for all her life lessons and love she shared in the midst of a overwhelming struggle as a single Mother.

Thank you Mama. I thank all my family, friends and everyone who took time to read and feel me.

1Love

Contents

A Name

If I could give you a name maybe It could be butterfly, or the moon that owns the midnight sky. If I could give you a name maybe it would be my Nightingale or maybe my wishing well. If I could give you a name, could it be waterfall, or maybe beautiful one who leaves me in awe. If I could give you a name! How about silk, or maybe sweet honey milk.

If I could give you a name, maybe soft whisper! Maybe flower on the River. Maybe I can call you just my Love, because this world doesn't describe my Queen enough.

Writer: Curtis Jones

Love is the Master of desire and author of deception, and those that yearn to feel its touch will always know confusion. Author: Curtis Jones

A Question

I once had a question about love and where it was, can I find this gift from above? I had a foolish idea that love has no fault, but life is a lesson and we all must be taught. I had a question could love really be understood? I never found the answer though I wish I could. I ask has my quest for love made me its prey, a naïve fly on a web that can't escape. I ask myself, was love a fairytale or just a big lie! I can't seem to get an answer! So I just cry.

My tears yearn for that which time has denied, with each passing day it becomes harder to hide. I question myself why my heart is like an open book, sometimes I feel so helpless, because I always get took. I desire to be studied pass my cover, so I can be loved and not just a lover.

Even with all my pain, disappointment and hurts, I know love is out there so I'll continue my search.

Author: Curtis Jones

About You

When I think about you, I see a forest of sweet fruit. I can almost taste the nectar of a plums center. The earth slowly swallows the rain which has soaked it. I can hear flutters of a Humming birds soft Wings. I imagine my love for you stronger than a legion of lions. My passion is as loud as the roar of waves pounding against a rocky shore.

When I think about you my words tangle my tongue, and my heart grips my soul and demands mercy. Most of all, I feel not even the threat of death and the graves call, shall separate the life line you supply my essence. Deny me my love and I shall take my wings as a dove and ride the final sun ray.

Author: Curtis Jones

Absence of Love

In the absence of love, I lost my way! Loneliness imprisoned my heart and would not release me.

I counted every second, minute and hour, because love always left my heart sick and my mouth sour.

Absence is such a cold, empty, dark still place, if love could be bought I would surely pay.

Instead I dream of a future with green grass, yet I wonder how long my absence of love shall last.

Author: Curtis Jones

Battle for my Mind

Sometimes twisted, sometimes sadistic and even unrealistic, my mind is a Battle Field of psychological Missiles. Bombs of burden exploding on every plain, LORD help me not to go down in the fire flames.

What's mine has never been so hard to keep! I don't want much just a peaceful sleep. This battle for my mind is taken its' toll, I hear the laughter of Satan tugging my soul. Everyone needs a rock so that's what I display, I smile out loud but I'll crack any day.

If you ask death a question he'll answer, even if you run he will eventually catch you. If GOD wasn't who he said, I know his Mercy is keeping from being dead. How can anyone be in a battle and not feel its sting, I've been lied on! betrayed, lost, Yet I remain!

No matter how many battles I lose I know the war isn't over yet.

Author: Curtis Jones

'Birdie Bye'

I'm watching two birds in a cage, I'M not sure of either's age. Both are white with light blue and speckles of grey. Yellow beaks and baby black eyes, I wonder if they cry?

Every morning I hear them chirping, but are they happy are hurting. Why are we the species that see something beautiful, catch it and make it do what we want it to do.

Why do you think something wants to be imprisoned and controlled, when freedom is desired for every living Soul. Sometimes I see the birds jumping, flapping and screaming loud, I know why, they just want out, but we think they want a finger in their mouth. Sometimes I come in and they are cuddled quietly together as to say, Will you Please open the cage and let us fly away.

Author: Curtis Jones

Broken Promises

I was so tired of telling myself this is the last hit, almost every day I promised I would quit. Wondering the streets at night I wanted this urge to leave me, but crack had a hold that wouldn't let me free. So many promises to family and my friends, only GOD knew how much I wanted this addiction to end.

Don't judge me because you're on the outside looking in, but cast the first stone if you have no sin. Well enough of what I use to be, because I once was blind but now I see. Now I'm saved sanctified and delivered from crack, with the Holy ghost in me and GOD leading I'm never going back.

Author: Curtis Jones

Death

Death blew me a kiss, but I refused to let it touch my lips. Death tried to speak into my ear, but I refused to listen to Its' fear. Death tried to seduce me and hold me in the night, it crept in my bed and held me tight.

Death placed a blanket over my eyes, nose and mouth, I locked every door and it still broke into my house. God told death to give me a head start in this race, at least when it took me, I had tasted GOD's grace.

Author: Curtis Jones

Don't Look Back

Don't look back when you walk out the door, because if you do it will hurt even more. Don't stop to explain, don't tell me why, if you're going to leave just say goodbye.

I love you, I need you, but I can make it alone, I want you, I'll miss you but I'll hold my own. But I can't tie you down, you got to be free, and I can't make you love one, just me. So don't look back I'll tell you again, just kiss me good bye baby cause this is the end.

Author: Curtis Jones

Echoes

No where to run or hide in fear, why can't I stop these echoes in my ears. I'm trying to let go but they continue to say why. I'm trying to be strong, but they say continue to cry.

As I sit and try to forget, no where to run from the hurt or hide from the fear. My heart says yes but my mind says no. which will hurt more I don't know, BANG! I'm dead, no more echoes.

Author: Curtis Jones

Emotional Trip

This is a silent shout, because no one knows what I'm talking about. I can't explain what I don't understand, I laugh and smile and still a sad man. Love seems to be a temporary fix, I don't know why, that's just it. Communication is the key, but no one can feel the loneliness in me.

God makes every soul unique, sometimes my emptiness feels so deep. True happiness only comes from within, but that's a bunch of bull somebody telling. I look at myself every day, and ask GOD to help me to help someone today, but can I get a little help this way or do I have a debt I still need to pay. Why is my pen my best friend, maybe it's the only thing that can figure out what I'm writing!

Sometimes I don't want to touch, and sometimes I feel Like I don't get enough. I think I'm having a talk to myself, I think this has been a real Emotional Trip.

Author Curtis Jones

Empty Bottle

I pick my pen up and take control, because it only lives when someone takes hold. Sometimes the colors bleed red, black or blue, it's strange how a blank page can reflect pieces of you. Can what you write be how you truly feel, it's the loudest thing in my life that nobody hears. Maybe they don't care! I'm just tired of being here.

Is there real love that last a complete cycle, or does it slowly dimmer like a burning candle. A true poet knows hope is a source of peace, a real fool holds on to a bottle that's empty.

Author: Curtis Jones

Find My Way Back

Lately I feel my life is adrift, I'm falling, tumbling down off a cliff. So many things that seem out of control, am I losing my existence? Am I losing my soul? For every answer another question arise, why can't I make everything go away as I close my eyes. Once things were certain, now so unsure, LORD I've strayed from you and become impure.

How empty I feel LORD only you know, If only I could cry but I'm afraid to let it show. I've allowed neglect of my needs lure me into sin, Please GOD! Help me find my way back again.

Author: Curtis Jones

Forgotten

People record the wrong you accomplish and erase the right, life is just a well I fell in last night. You can climb the wall and break your nails but no one can hear you at the bottom. We lay in this dark, hopeless hole of despair, stale air everywhere. We grasp for hope and receive no hands, it's like I have been forgotten.

Depression is our guest and fear is our chair. This represents my world of lonely nights, cruel days and doubt! I looked every day for a way out. In the midst of my thoughts, I looked up and realized there was a light at the top of the well,

And a voice yelled, just when you thought you were forgotten!

Author: Curtis Jones

Fruitful Candy Love

The thing I miss most is your kiss of sweet honey lickerish, and your tasty milk of chocolate. The slow nibble over your round plums and the cherry juice I taste under my tongue. A strawberry banana split, hot marshmallow just melted! Can you hear the chestnuts cracking?

This is a lunch on love cinnamon buns with icing on top! do you feel what I'm talking about? I smell your apricots! Can I snicker your bar and chew, and blow some big bubbles with you. Let me sample your candy apple rum, you're invited so come. I'm at border line of having enough, I'm lying! Just give me my Fruitful candy love.

Author: Curtis jones

Gold Coin

Once there was a woman who wanted to be rich, and didn't care what it took to get. One day as she strolled by a beautiful pond, She spotted a object on the ground round Like a coin. She picks it up an says, it's just a dirty old quarter, then she takes it and tosses it in the water. Several days later a Woman was swimming across that same pond, an saw a shiny object on the bottom. She reaches down an holds it to the sun, thank you Jesus someone lost a gold coin.

Author: Curtis Jones

Hall Ways

Hallways have so many doors that sometimes lead to another hall, some lead to rooms full of junk, and some rooms are empty and dark. Hallways are locked sometimes so you can't enter but some open so you can exit. Hallways can be so loud you can't hear anything but noise, and some can be so silent lonely and void.

Hallways can be so distant you see no end and so short you wish it were longer. Hallways can lead you to everything you want, and some to nothing you need. I'm describing life and all the directions and questions it gives. Despite of all its' uncertainly the hallway to Heaven is the best answer.

Author: Curtis Jones

Holding Back the Tears

As I reminisce in my loves past, so many times I wanted it to last. Sometimes it's not so easy to let go, sometimes it's not so easy letting your emotions show. Hurt is something, but we can do without it, sooner or later it's something we all will get. My poems help me to express my more sensitive side, that part of me I attempt to hide. I heard it takes a real man to break down and cry, not sure if it's true or is it a lie.

But I have learned, if love is not in your heart it's easy not to cry, without love you will be miserable until time passes bye. I finally understand after all these years! no matter how strong you are, you can't hold back the tears!

Author: Curtis jones

I Need A Listen

Touch me ,hear me, see me, ,I'm real! understand me, free me, I'm here I'm wondering about me, I'm scared of me and only GOD knows what I mean. I'm dying slowly and so empty, can someone give me and stop taking.

I'm tired and so lonely in this room, did I mention it was cold. I hear my heart beat and I hear voices in my head talking! Am I really crazy? I don't know what to say so don't expect an answer. It's dark in here but light shines from time to time, but I can't step It's a too wet sign. I laugh and smile but just to deceive, because that's what everyone needs me to be.

My journals have no canal to end, I'm writing this so don't pour in. I don't need a lesson! I need a listen.

Author: Curtis Jones

'Inner Reflection'

Trapped in a circle with no cracks, did I mention it was dark and I don't know where I'm at. I need someone because I'm alone and cold, I just want someone in my world to trust and hold.

This life is so cruel and full of deceit, I know how to love but can somebody know how to love me. In case there is a mystery in my expression, I just want to open my heart with no deception.

Gimme someone who takes my body to places of infatuation, Someone who I don't mind time wasting. Oh well, maybe I'm just a dreamer searching for fools' gold, LORD help me to find peace in my empty soul.

Author: Curtis Jones

Just Blind

I told you, you needed someone else in your life, because I knew I would never treat you right. You deserve more than to wait for me to come home, you don't need a Child you need someone grown! I know you said you would wait for me to change, but I've been a player to long in this game.

Being with more than one is all I've ever done! I don't think I've ever been in love with anyone. For once I think something happening inside of me, could this be the reason I feel empty. Now that you're gone I cry sometime, damn! Maybe I was falling and was just too blind.

Author: Curtis Jones

'Last Night'

Last night I had a nightmare!! that you vanished from life somewhere. There was a clinch in my chest that stole my breath, and there was a fall in my heart like a bottomless cliff.

It felt like a demon pulling my soul mate away, I plead to heaven and challenged hell each day. You're more precious than a ruby at the bottom of the sea, and your lips are like rose pedals just blowing. The venom in your arms seemed to paralyze me, your legs are like a WIDOWS WEB wrapped around me.

Back to last night because it was not what it seemed, suddenly my eyes popped open and my nightmare was just a dream.

PLEASE DON'T EVER LEAVE!!!

Author: Curtis Jones

Last Song

Well here we are doing what we thought would never come, my hands slip from your finger tips ,because it's time go. i'm trapped inside your beautiful ruby eyes, stop baby! you're not the only one going to cry. what's going to happen as I turn my back! Will be a pain sharper than a hearts' attack! A bye has never been good, so please don't whisper turn around if you could.

The sweet melody of your love symphony, i'm letting you play for me. You have given me when I couldn't do the same! I hope and pray this won't be the last song we sang.

Author: Curtis Jones

Lonely Tree

It's spring and I'm leaving again,

Should I plant my roots or branch into the wind.

Sometimes I feel so alive, sometimes I feel so dry.

Sometimes the sun shines and sometimes rain makes me cry. I lean
to the North, South, West and East, When I fall no one hears me.

I help those who need shelter but people cut at me, I'm lost in the
forest!! I'm a lonely tree.

Author: Curtis Jones

Lost and Lonely

I would ask you not to cry if I could, even though you hurt and feel you should. I enjoyed my life as GOD allowed me to stay, life is a journey and soon we must come this way. Once time is gone your time has been spent, don't wait to long and wonder where the time all went. Trust GOD when you can't trust your heart, because grief held to long only tears you a part. A test is only part of your testimony, GOD never leaves you even when you feel lost and Lonely.

Author: Curtis Jones

Love

As I sit here in this shadows' mystery, I ask a question of love and its' history! Is Love the soul of a hearts' chariot? Or is it the immortal surge of desires buried. Love is so evasive and yet so rarely understood, I'm like a fallen tree laying in the woods.

OHH GOD! My plea I now set free, why must this yearning continue to torment me.

I run to it, I look for it, I hide from it, I hate it, I need it, I love it. Confusion is a trademark of Loves' footprint, LOVE! is man truly equipped to handle it.

Author: Curtis Jones

Me

Searching for an answer within my mind, pedals of a flower falling in time. The reality of life or the fantasy of a dream, nothing in my life is the way it seems. The sea of eternity that has no bounds, this wall in my mind that releases no sound! Crying to escape, I often flee, but there is no escape, because the wall is me. It's like looking into a mirror that doesn't reflect, like pieces of a puzzle that never connect. There's more to my presence than what you can see, how can you know when I don't know me.

My purpose in life I wish to understand, I have love and life but still a lost man. Maybe someday I will find the key, until then I will just be me.

Author: Curtis Jones

Morning Kiss

I woke up this morning before she did, and I rolled over to kiss her forehead. Her face looked so peaceful and perfect to me, so I wrapped my arms around you and squeezed. I love your soft sensual body close to me, I love watching my Queen as she sleeps. I've never known any woman who makes me feel this way, will you be my right now, tomorrow and yesterday. With you I'm complete and whole, I promise to never let you grow old alone. Let me be your knight that brightens your day, I'm like your Burger King you can have me your way!

Author: Curtis Jones

My Book

Just to know this life isn't just an empty chest, I want to open this box and know love's caress. This portal in my soul is like a black hole, this pulling and longing is grasping for control. Give me eyes that look beyond my face, give me hands that touch my heart and not below my waist. Just stand in my presence and feel my space, my thoughts are running and I'm tired of this race.

I long to live and not just exist, lord give me somebody who understands this. A smile can only hold sadness for so long, I want to begin my life with a poetic psalms. Last night I had a dream I was awake, but my passion was dying and lying in a grave.

Then I said death and despair shall not be my final look, but peace and hope shall be the author of my book!

Author: Curtis jones

My Bunk

This is a place my body seldom finds sleep, how can I with cold hard steel below and above me.

All I want is to roll in a spot of peace of mind, but my bunk is designed to punish with its claws of iron.

Author: Curtis Jones

My Love

31

My love I'd never thought you would come my way, If you are a dream I refuse to wake. My Love you are my fantasy and my ecstasy, you're my tender, my Love and my Queen.

Can a tale be told without a story, the ink of my tongue has published a book of your glory! The sun could not equal the brilliance of your smile, You are my center that makes my life worth while.

My Love you're my mirror that causes me to reflect, you're my missing piece that my rib connects. may the spirit of GOD blow upon us and never leaves us alone.

My love if a word could describe you, it would be, where the sunset meets the moon light, I'd call you infinity. I seal our love with the blood of our entwined soul, may the spirit of GOD blow upon us and never leave us alone.

Author: Curtis Jones

My Queen

I just took a walk and suddenly felt blue, because I realize the sky reminds of you. My eyes have beheld many glorious scenes, but none has held me in awe as much as my Queen. Her voice is like the soft song of a saxophone, her eyes are a palace and her lips are a majestic throne.

Your skin has the feel of the finest of luxurious silk, with a tasty kiss sweet as honey, dates, and buttermilk. Your love is like a wet rain that waters a dry ground, and your beauty transcends the Heavens and even beyond.

No sea is deep enough to find such a precious pearl! I kneel humbly before your royalty and ask to share my world. I ask you to wear my ring as your king ,share my heart, my love and be my queen.

Author: Curtis jones

My Sax

Excuse me as I begin to play with my Saxophone! It's not my intension to break your concentration and draw your attention, but you can still listen. I'm about to take it in my hands and wrap my lips around the rim. O yeah! I'm keeping it clean, so stay away from the obscene. Because I'm about to blow real slow down this black and gold hole, and create such a silky, sensual hypnotic flow, your mind can't phantom and your body can't let go. I'm talking about music that touches your essence and gives you affection from the fingers of vibration, and sound connection that erects the unexpected. I'm sorry if I've gone to fast let me break the tempo, I've tried to fertilize your imagination into growth. Without perversion I was a tender surgeon so relax! I'm finished playing my Sax.

Author: Curtis Jones

'My Time'

I'm a individual with a broad imagination, but I can only handle so much frustration.

This cycle I seem to be entwined, when can I feel it's my time?

A hopeless romantic at heart but why, to know true love I yearn before I die.

I want love, passion and excitement, I try to pretend but I'm not content.

Once I took, Then I gave, now I need, I feel like a prisoner who can't be freed.

I'm sorry if I committed some type of crime, but GOD I feel I've served my time.

I never knew how strong this craving could be, will this aching gone on for eternity?

Between Love and Hate there's a thin line, I hate love because it won't give me my time..

Author: Curtis Jones

My World

I'm staring at the cracked walls, in my world there's nothing at all but captivity, the loneliness and peace is slowly eating at me. This dark holes void is my friend, fangs of a viper biting at my skin. The footsteps of a key! In my world is captivity. The echoes of chaos peaking at my mind, the lights in my heart but my eyes are blind. I rewrite my memories, because I hate my future, my dreams are nightmares and full of torture. If my world sounds sad then you see my vision.

There's numbness in my tongue but you need to listen. I hear a cold breeze blowing out the walls hole! I feel the hands of the reaper ripping at my soul. A black crow is cawing backwards I don't understand, I'm a chained animal! I thought I was a man. My silent screams are the tears on my cheeks, The ball head mirror man is staring at me.

In my world the circle can't be broken, my breath is being squeezed and I'm slowly choking. My song is dying no need for crying. Close your eyes real tight, because no one will find you. My world just came to a end.

Author: Curtis Jones

'Never'

I never had a plan B because my A meant always,

I never thought my heart would need a Band-aid.

I never thought your whisper was a soft lie,

I never thought I'd ever be writing this letter goodbye.

You are a thief that stole a part of my life,

I never thought I'd be crying on my pillows at night.

Loving you was wrong but I thought it was alright,

My so called friends laughed behind my back.

it's all good, because I'm glad I figured you out now, so I don't look stupid asking about how. Sometimes just listen to the lesson life is teaching, just learn to let wisdom rule while you're reaching.

Author Curtis Jones

Players

37

Thinking back over the countless hearts I've used, I think of why and become confused. The pretending and lies I often recall, so many hearts that took the fall.

Often I just wanted to say no, why I did not I don't know. Was it the obsession of just making love, as I lay in my bed and looked off above!

Players only wish to please themselves! They play with hearts and put them on shelves. But players pay the price for all their sins, because they always have nothing in the end!

Author: Curtis Jones

Quotes by Curtis

Love and lust run such a tight race that not even wisdom can tell the winner, yet time always does!

If GOD holds your future! Why can't you learn from your past!

We are the last to know GOD's plan and the first to mess it up.

Love with no meaning is the same as a sad song that never ends.

Love without passion is the loneliest feeling of all.

Pure love is something fallen men will never have.

When water overflows we witness a water fall, when a heart overflows we witness falling in love.

If love is like a virus! I pray I never get well!

When you sing to GOD he will open the ear in your heart.

Talk alone and you're crazy, talk crazy to people and you're crazy, if you keep silent you're crazy, GOD knows you don't have to speak to be heard.

Author: Curtis Jones

Raining Outside

It's raining outside, I can't feel it inside. It's dripping from the edge of the roof, and it's dripping from my eyes to. It's raining outside I can't hear a sound. I see it falling and splashing on the ground. I see it rolling from my windows pain! I wonder when it will rain again. It's raining outside, I can't feel it inside.

It's after midnight with fog, I'm writing this poem in the dark. I'm letting my heart guide my hand, I'm all alone and my shadow is my friend. I see an angel watching over me, lord this jail is hell! Please set me free.

It's raining outside, I want to feel it on my face one time!

Author: Curtis Jones

Still reaching

I'm needing but I'm still reaching, I'm reaping and weeping but I'm still reaching. I'm tired and sleepy but I'm still reaching. I'm hurting but still reaching, lonely but I'm still reaching. I've given my all but I'm still reaching. I've been left but I'm still reaching,

I'm forgetting but I'm still reaching. I'm still crying but I'm still reaching. I'm still in love but I'm still reaching, I'm saved but still reaching. I don't know sometimes if I'm still leaving, but Heaven I'm still reaching.

Author: Curtis Jones

'*Stop*'

Stop, because your Love has consumed me, like a thief you've stolen my heart completely. A man was meant to have some restraint, but when it comes to you boo, I just can't.

I say STOP! But I really want you to keep going, because I hate saying no because I love what you are doing. Your eyes are like a black hole pulling me into its grip, Your kiss is like a honey tree dripping on my lips.

Your voice is like a warm breeze blowing across the ocean, and your sensuous walk cast a spell like a witches' potion. The Loving you give my body has no definition, Not a dictionary can describe this blissful feeling you're giving.

If you study the stars sometimes you'll see one drop, God bless our love and I pray we never STOP.

Author: Curtis Jones

'The Porch'

Old porch with dry wood,

Crack between the pieces that show dirt.

Cried on it, smiled on it and kissed,

Laid on it, stood on it and pissed.

Squeaky steps and Mosquito bites.

Claimed cars that pass bye

Where my brothers and I use to fight,

This Porch before the street lights,

Everyday I stepped to the edge,

I wish you would Mama said.

Author: Curtis Jones

'The Puppy'

43

I once saw a puppy born, Black silky fur it adorned.

I'm a Small child but poor. The little puppy was left all alone barking.

It was crying and so was I. His Mother abandoned him with maggots in his eyes. I never saw anything going to die.

It kept barking loudly as if to scare death away and softly fading. No poor child should see this Death.

The puppy lay without motion. I stood still wiping my tears, listening to one last sigh for help. I'm grown but sometimes I still hear those hopeful echoes hark, and I cry.

Author: Curtis Jones

The Rain

As I stand in the rain and look up at the sky, I recall the day we bitterly said good bye. It was a rainy one like today, when I cursed you out and turned away. My heart hurts from my foolish mistake, like yours was when I said my love was fake. I know I said I could live without you, but now that you're gone, I don't know what to do.

I remember your eyes filled with many tears, if time were reversed I would have you here. As I gaze upon a rainy white dove! My heart cries out to you my love! I thought the rain was supposed to leave a bright rainbow! for me it only brings back my sorrow.

WHY MUST I FEEL ALL THIS SCORN AND PAIN, SOMETIMES I WISH

THERE WAS NO DAMN RAIN.

Author: Curtis jones

The River

45

I'm standing on the bank of this river, as it races by snatching every piece of debris it can. I'm watching the dark sand beneath being slowly torn from the earth. They say the faster a river flows the closer you are to where the water falls off the edge. The longer I stand in this spot, the more of a chance the sediment will calapse and I'll be pulled off on the rocks that await me. Sin is the exact way the longer you stand on the edge watching, the more you increase your chances to fall into it.

Author: Curtis Jones

This Room

8 x 12ft, cold steel toilet with a sink, Metal bunks, some light, noise, can't think.

Hot by nature, artic freezer, joints stiff, guards cruel, mates denied, racism, ass sniff.

This room, solid rock, piss corner, Lockdown, single occupant, 3 bro 3 foreigners.

False charges, frustration, phone calls no, 3 fights, protection, accused, Pauls' bro.

Crying, pleading, injustice, praying, Kneeling, standing, crawling, laying! This room, echoes, darkness, and hides, Pain, suffering, tears, deep inside.

See no reps, promised help, no hands, Guards cruel, careless, laugh, I'm still a man.

Madness, chances none, lied on, stay, LORD! Help me leave this room today.

Author: Curtis Jones

This Space

47

There is an echo sounding in my heart, because Love has no space. The water of silent drips splash like tears, do you know how it feels. The roar of emptiness is like the coldness of winter, GOD this space is so lonely but you know, my veins are highways flowing from the center of my soul. Hold the night from my eyes so that I behold the divine gift of Loves' affection.

Not through flesh but by faith so it lights my path, then my empty space shall be filled at last.

Author: Curtis Jones

Tired

I'm tired of being hurt and not hugged, I'm tired of being left and not loved. I'm tired of wiping tears and wanting trust, I'm tired of words void and whispers rush.

I'm tired of harsh encounters and empty hearts, I'm tired of lavish lips and laughing departs. I'm tired of watching sunsets and wanting sunrise, I'm tired of painful touches and silent cries.

I'm tired of broken spirits and boasting souls, I'm tired of wooden tokens and loneliness hold.

Writer: Curtis Jones

Twisted

I never claim to be more than I am and I never claim to have more than I have. I never claim I always make the right choice, but when I scream no one hears my voice. People always see what they want to hear, Sometimes my mind gets so twisted but they don't seem to care. I'm a private garbage can! Just dump on me, I'm like broken glass they step over me.

I'm not a rock I can be broke, but I trust GOD sometimes to give me hope. People say how you were but GOD told me who I am, People judge and criticize but GOD forgave and didn't condemn. I still hurt sometimes and I feel pain, but GOD has straightened my twisted life and left me changed.

Author: Curtis Jones

Water on the Hands

Trust is what you wanted but I never earned it,

Love was what you needed but I never learned it.

There is something you said that I finally understand,

No matter how much you say I'm sorry it will never wash the water off your hands.

Writer: Curtis Jones

What I Want

I want to be loved by someone who is truly real! I want to be loved by someone who understands how I feel. I don't want a relationship devised of just making love, I want a relationship when I'm know I'm loved. I mean I want a relationship with love not all lust, a relationship I can take my time and not rush.

I want a relationship where I'm respected and trusted, not a relationship where someone runs to your face and say I've been busted. I want a relationship when I know I am loved. If your love seems to be fading away, don't keep me hanging on just come out and say. It's better to have loved and lost, than to never have loved at all.

Author: Curtis Jones

When

When did you give up on this love, when was your last cry that said enough? Was it when I'd get lost going on the way to the store, was it when I said it wouldn't happen no more. When was the last time you looked out the window? Yelling please will you to stop banging on the door. When was the last time we had laid in bed, When was the last time you longed just to be held?

I had eyes but just couldn't see, I was losing the best thing ever happened to me. It's a cliché , but you never miss a good thing till it's gone, Now I'm empty and feel so lost and alone, When was it a lie when you said you didn't care, I know the truth now because you're not here.

A heart can love for only so long, now I understand baby because I did you so wrong. You don't have to guess I'm in an emotional storm, I guess this is why this is such a sad song.

Author: Curtis Jones

Word in the Wind

As the word was cast upon the shoulder of the wind, life has been and shall be. Creation hails for its' power of change and growth, the wind is GODS' Spirit that carries the seed of the word. It blows to and fro to feed the birds, the trees, the flowers, the seas, Man, the dead, the living, the proud, the willing.

The word in the wind whistles, rains, thunders and proclaim that GOD is present, though unseen he is what was and shall be. LISTEN to the word in the wind, stop and listen again.

Author: Curtis Jones

'Yo Dance'

Baby love when I think about yo dance, I'm talking about more than the motion of your soft sensual body in display, twisting and shaking. I'll start explaining! It's the way you moved slowly into my thoughts before I saw you . I even knew the way your vibes moved me before we actually meet. Yo dance is your graceful presence and your unforgettable and breathe taking face. Yo dance is every groove and every curve of your silhouette, your silky smooth skin, your Beautiful eyes that captivate, your soft sweet speech, the way you wrap your arms around me and even a leg while I go to sleep, and the way you say I love Baby, You feel me? I know you can, because I just described why I love to see Yo dance.

Author: Curtis Jones

Your Way

The saddest thing in life is when you don't want to live, and the saddest thing in love is when you don't want to give.

When someone has stolen what should be saved, and all you do is lay in bed like a grave. When all you desire are flies on your face, and you pray GOD will take your breath away.

I just shared a heart break and I hope it never comes your way.

Author: Curtis Jones